WOMEN
IN HISTORY

WOMEN AND WORK

Patricia Owen

Wayland

WOMEN
IN HISTORY

Women and Business
Women and Education
Women and Literature
Women and Politics
Women and Science
Women and Sport
Women and the Arts
Women and the Family
Women and War
Women and Work

Series Editor: Amanda Earl
Consultant: Deirdre Beddoe BA, PhD, Dip Ed,
Reader in History at the Polytechnic of Wales
Designer: Joyce Chester
Picture Editor: Liz Miller

Front Cover: Women workers during the First World War resurfacing a road.

Back Cover: Top left – Women working in a bicycle factory in 1895. Top right – Matchgirls on strike outside the Bryant and May factory in 1888. Bottom left – Munition workers during the First World War. Bottom right – General and Municipal Workers' Union members join the Trades Union Congress workers' march in 1975.

First published in 1989 by
Wayland (Publishers) Limited
61 Western Road, Hove
East Sussex, BN3 1JD
England

© Copyright 1989 Wayland (Publishers) Limited

British Library Cataloguing in Publication Data
Owen, Patricia
  Women and work. – (Women in history)
  1. Great Britain. Women. Employment,
  ca 1740 –1990 – for schools
  I. Title II. Series
  331.4'0941

  ISBN 1– 85210–387– 6

Typeset by: Lizzie George, Wayland
Printed in Italy by G. Canale & C.S.p.A., Turin
Bound in the UK by Mac Lehose & Partners, Portsmouth

Picture acknowledgements
The pictures in this book were supplied by the following: Barnaby's Picture Library 44 (above); BBC Hulton Picture Library 26, 34, 40; BPCC/Aldus Archive 4, 7 (right), 9 (below by permission of Master & fellows, Trinity College, Cambridge), 12 (right), 19, 20, 22; Bridgeman Art Library 9 (above); Daisy Noakes 21; ET Archives 7 (left), 24; Format 36 (below), 38, 41, 42, 43 (both); The Mansell Collection 10, 13, 16, 17; Mary Evans Picture Library 5 (above), 6, 8, 11, 12 (left), 15, 17, 23; Topham Picture Library 19, 25, 28, 29, 30 (both), 31, 32 (both), 35, 36 (above), 42 (above), 44 (below). The remaining pictures are from the Wayland Picture Library. The artwork on pages 33 and 41 was supplied by Thames Cartographic Services.

Permissions
The publishers would like to thank the following for permitting the use of extracts from their publications:
A & C Black for *Where We Used to Work* by K. Hudson, 1980; Age Exchange Publications for *What did you do in the War, Mum?* by Margaret Kippin, 1985; The Bodley Head for *Women and a Changing Civilization* by Winifred Holtby, 1934; Collins Publishers for *Equal at Work? Women in Men's Jobs* by A. Coote, 1979; Croom Helm for *Women Workers in the First World War* by G. Braybon, 1981; Daisy Noakes and QueenSpark Books for *The Town Beehive – a young girl's lot, Brighton 1910–34*, 1975; Edward Arnold for *Life in the Industrial Revolution* by P. Bartley, 1987; Fontana for *Women at War* by Arthur Marwick, 1977; Gower Publishing for *The Chartists* by D. Thompson, 1984; Hutchinson for *Women and Work* by Ross Davies, 1975; Methuen & Co. for *A People's War* by Peter Lewis, 1986; *Options* magazine for the quote by Steve Penneck, July 1987; Penguin Books for *Child Care and the Growth of Love* by J. Bowlby, 1953 and *Strong Minded Women* by J. Horowitz Murray, 1984; Peter Owen for *Women at the Top, Achievement and Family Life* by J. Wheeler Bennett, 1977; Pluto Press for the poem 'The Women's Labour' by Mary Collier, from *Hidden from History* by Sheila Rowbotham, 1973; Purnell Books for *Below Stairs* (1968) and *My Mother and I* (1972) by Margaret Powell; *Spare Rib* magazine for the use of an extract from issue number 45, page 17; Unwin Hyman for *Time and Tide Wait for No Man* by Dale Spender, 1984; Virago Press for *Bombers and Mash: The Domestic Front 1939–45* by Raynes Minns, 1980.

Contents

Above This wood cut shows a woman silk worker in the seventeenth century. Women worked in many trades, either with their husbands or as business-women in their own right.

'

*When evening does approach
    we homeward hie
And our domestic toils
    incessant plie;
. . . Bacon and Dumpling in the
    pot we boil.
Our beds we make, our swine
    to feed the while . . .
Early next morning we on you
    attend;
Our children dress and feed,
    their Cloths we mend;
And in the Field our daily Task
    renew. . .*
Mary Collier, *The Women's Labour*, 1739.

'

Introduction

What kind of work did women do one, two or three hundred years ago? Was their work very different from the work done by women today? This book examines in detail the vast variety of work done by women from the eve of the Industrial Revolution to the present day.

It evaluates working-class women's contribution to industry and describes the involvement of women in the formation and growth of trade unions. The difficulties faced by middle-class women in the mid-nineteenth century, in their attempts to enter professions such as medicine and teaching, are also highlighted.

The book examines the effects of the First and Second World Wars, which not only helped to increase women's job opportunities, but also gave them a taste of independence. In post-war Britain, women in employment have continued to campaign for legislation which will promote equal opportunities and equal pay for women at work.

The idea that jobs, both paid and unpaid, should be divided into 'women's work' and 'men's work' is sometimes called the 'sexual division of labour'. This means that simply because they are born female, women are presumed to be good at certain work – cleaning, cooking, looking after people, caring for children, and at doing delicate, fiddly, boring and monotonous jobs. If a woman does go out to work, she is assumed to be less committed to her job than a man, and is expected to 'fit in' her work alongside looking after a home and family.

Women in Britain have won acceptance of the idea that they are entitled to the right to work on equal terms with men, and – theoretically at least – to be paid the same for doing the same job. Single and childless women who are determined and prepared to overcome opposition and prejudice now have far more opportunities for doing interesting, responsible and well-paid jobs than their mothers or grandmothers would ever have dreamed of. However, to be truly equal with men at work most women with dependants still find they have to be prepared to work on men's terms, putting their jobs before family life.

1

Eve of the Industrial Revolution

1760–1800

It is often mistakenly believed that women's involvement in work came about mainly as a result of the Industrial Revolution, when women could actually be seen to go out to work. However, this is a false picture. Throughout history women have worked to feed and clothe themselves and their dependants.

In the sixteenth and seventeenth centuries, women in country villages played an important part in the production of goods. Those involved in the production of textiles, such as woollen cloth and silk, were regarded as skilled craftswomen. In towns, during this period, women worked as shopkeepers or in various other trades, together with their husbands and families, or as business-women in their own right. Their trades included the brewing and selling of ale, and the selling of vegetable produce at markets. Women were also very much valued for their work as healers and skilled midwives.

Until the late eighteenth century, most people in Britain still

Above Before the Industrial Revolution women spun wool by hand.

> Memorandum, That I Elizabeth Bence, Daur. of Peter Bence, late of the Parish of St. James, Westmr [Westminster] . . . Do put myself Apprentice to Ann Jaquin, Citizen and Goldsmith of London for the Term of Seven Years from this Day there being paid to my said mistress Thirty Pounds.
>
> Goldsmiths' Company Apprenticeship Book, 1747.

Left The profession of midwife was originally entirely in the hands of skilled women. Later, however, they had to overcome great difficulties in order to be accepted by men into the medical profession.

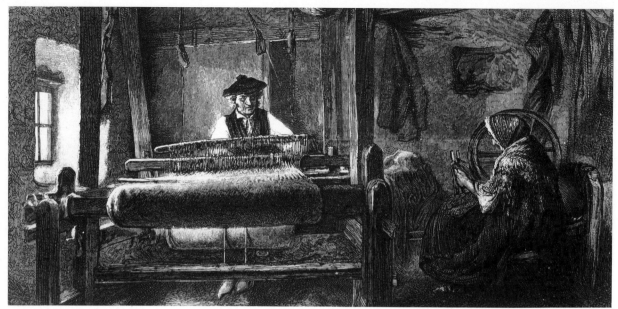

Above Before the Industrial Revolution weaving was done at home in small workshops by the whole family.

‘▬▬▬▬

Day labourers, who whilst they are employed abroad them-selves, get 40 or 50 pounds of wool at a time, to employ their wives and children at home in carding and spinning. . . Daniel Defoe, *Remarks upon Mr Webber's Scheme and the Draper's Pamphlet*, 1741.

▬▬▬▬’

‘▬▬▬▬

I have known instances of the wife's management of livestock, together with the earnings of herself and children in haytime, and harvest, etc., produce nearly as much money in the course of the year, as her husband by all his labour during the same time. Political Enquiry into the Consequences of Enclosing Waste Lands, 1785.

▬▬▬▬’

lived in the countryside. From early childhood, girls from poor families were used to looking after animals and doing heavy farm work. It was also common for a girl to become a 'live-in' farm servant at a large, wealthy house for six to seven years. Once they had a family of their own, women added to their food supplies by growing crops and, where possible, keeping a pig or cow. They would supplement this by doing seasonal work on a larger farm at harvest time.

Even women from richer families worked. Once married, they had to feed, care for and organize the work of their servants and employees. Most food and drink, such as bread, beer and honey, was produced at home, as were simple medicines, candles, and soap. Some women also ran their own dairies, and a few women farmers became famous for their successful experiments in improving crop yields.

Most women's work before the later part of the eighteenth century was based at home, or in small workshops. Women were able to combine their roles as mother and worker, and all members of the family, even children, worked together.

With the start of the Industrial Revolution (around the 1760s), and the invention of new machinery and methods of powering it, enormous changes took place in people's working lives. Now, many goods were beginning to be produced much more quickly and cheaply in the new factories than in the home or small workshop. The Industrial Revolution caused millions of people to move from the countryside to the growing towns and cities to look for work.

Apart from a few highly paid male supervisors, most of the workers in these new 'manufactories' were women and children, particularly so in the industries making textiles such as cotton and silk. Women were considered more suitable than men, especially since they could be paid much less. Among the girls who worked in the textile factories were 'pauper apprentices', the orphans, or children from very poor families who could not afford to keep them. They were sent to work in the mills for seven years or more, and were often hundreds of miles away from their families. They were treated little better than slaves, half starved, often beaten and locked up so they could not escape.

Not all poor women worked in the new factories, however. Some took in work at home. They made boxes or envelopes, did laundry or ironing. For this work, women were paid 'by the piece' for the work completed and not by an hourly rate. The wages for most homework were hardly enough to live on.

Needlework occupied many women. This was either done at home, or in crowded 'sweatshops'. When there was a rush of new orders from rich people – particularly if there was a royal wedding or funeral – women and girls had to work all night and day to get their work finished.

Plenty of women in the early years of the Industrial Revolution worked in jobs that were heavy, dirty and dangerous. Women worked in ironworks, as chain-and-nail makers, as brick workers, stone-breakers and in the mines. Women's contribution to the development of industry and manufacturing is indisputable.

'
A notice advertising a corn mill suitable for cotton spinning: 'The manufacturer may be supplied with plenty of hands at low wages as there are a great number of women, boys and girls, in the town of Ruthin that are out of employ . . .
Manchester Mercury *newspaper, 1787.*
'

Above A factory scene of 1840. Pauper apprentices had to put up with terrible, dangerous conditions. Notice the young child under the machine.

Left From the nineteenth century onwards, many women took in homework, rather than work in a factory. The pay was extremely bad.

Above Many women had to leave their new-born children to work in the 'manufactories'. Often babies were dosed with a drug containing opium to make them sleep while their mothers were away.

> *My mother worked in a manufactory from a very early age . . . she was married early. She became the mother of eleven children. As she recovered from her lying-in, so she went to work, the babe being brought to her at stated times to receive nourishment. . . I have known her, after the close of a hard day's work, to sit up nearly all night for several nights together washing and mending clothes* . . . Joseph Corbett, button burnisher, 1840.

2

The 'Problem' of Women Workers

c.1830–1860

As the Industrial Revolution continued into the early nineteenth century, women's paid work became easier to see as separate from the unpaid work such as child care, housework, cooking and washing which they did at home.

By 1861, over a quarter of the female population over the age of fifteen was working. Often women worked in factories for thirteen hours or more, making it hardly possible for them to combine paid work with caring for their families. Most women must have been too tired to do much housework when they came home from work. After 1847, Saturday afternoons became a half-day holiday, but Sunday was the only full day off work.

While mothers worked in the factories, their young babies had to be left with slightly older children, or with women unable to go out to work themselves. If possible, mothers fed their babies during the dinner break, but the crying, hungry babies were often dosed with a very strong addictive drug containing opium, called 'Godfrey's Cordial' or 'Infant Quietness', to keep them quiet. Many babies died from this treatment. The hardships facing women workers, especially mothers, were often used as an argument against women going out to work at all. However, they had no option. The old home-based system of working was just not economical in comparison with the new 'manufactories'.

Although hours were long and conditions difficult, there were some advantages for single women in the new working patterns of industrial Britain. Single women had some independence, could earn their own money and spend it as they wanted. Many people remarked on the spirit of freedom which single factory girls seemed to have. They were criticized for dressing in clothes that were too fancy for working girls, and for spending their precious free time in pubs or drinking clubs. For many families it was a last resort to send their daughters to the mill.

After 1833, children under the age of nine were barred from the textile mills. Alternative work for young girls in towns was to sell produce as street sellers. Girls as young as six years old sold flowers, watercress, matches or other cheap goods to passers by.

> **'**
> *There is no mistaking her in the streets. The long day's silence is made up for the moment she is free, by the loud and boisterous laughter . . . she is apparently born minus shyness . . .* Lettice Bell in *The Factory Girl*.
> **'**

Below *The way women dressed for work was often criticized during the nineteenth century, particularly the wearing of trousers! This picture from 1867 shows a girl working on the pit brow.*

In mining areas, however, both women and children continued to work underground until 1842. Mining had always been hard and dangerous work, but there was generally little choice of other local jobs. In 1842, a government report was issued, revealing and condemning all the terrible details of women's and children's work in the mines. Such an outcry followed that women were immediately stopped by law from working in the pits.

Laws such as the Mines Act were designed to protect women from harsh conditions. Other Acts of Parliament reduced women's working hours in the textile industry. Protective legislation, as it was called, stopped women from doing certain skilled jobs. So, although the legislation was supposedly aimed at reducing women's working hours and improving conditions of work, in fact it also limited the type of work women were legally allowed to do. Women's work seemed to be particularly limited in higher-paid jobs where they might be in competition with men.

The way women dressed for work was often criticized during the nineteenth century. The idea of women wearing 'men's' clothes such as trousers, even when they were obviously far safer and more convenient than skirts, was felt by some people at the time to be indecent and immoral. Trousers were sometimes called 'unmentionables' or 'non-talkaboutables', not at all the sort of thing 'nice' women would wear.

In spite of all the disapproval and concern voiced by middle-class society about women workers, and the effects that their working lives would have on their character and their family life, women had to work to keep body and soul together, they did not have a choice. During the nineteenth century, working-class women as well as men led busy, exhausting lives.

The Watercress Girl

In the 1850s, the historian Henry Mayhew collected information about the lives and work of some of London's poorest inhabitants, including street sellers. Here, a little girl who sold watercress tells her story: 'I go about the streets with water-creases (watercresses) crying, "Four bunches a penny, water-creases". I am just eight years old – that's all, and I've a big sister, and a brother and a sister younger than I am. . . Before that, I had to take care of a baby for my aunt. No, it wasn't heavy – it was only two months old; but I minded it for ever such a time – till it could walk. It was a very nice little baby, not a very pretty one; but, if I touched it under the chin, it would laugh.

'I used to go down to market along with another girl, as must be fourteen, 'cos she does her hair back up. When we've bought a lot [of watercress], we sits down on a doorstep, and ties up the bunches. We never goes home to breakfast till we've sold out; but, if it's very late, then I buys a penn'orth of pudden, which is very nice with gravy.

'It's very cold before winter comes on reg'lar – specially getting up of a morning. I gets up in the dark by the light of the lamp in the court. I bears the cold – you must; so I puts my hands under my shawl, though it hurts 'em to take hold of the creases, especially when we takes 'em to the pump to wash 'em. No; I never see any children crying – it's no use.

'Sometimes I make a great deal of money. One day I took 1s. 6d., and the creases cost 6d.; but it isn't often I get such luck as that. I oftener makes 3d. or 4d. than 1s. I always give my mother my money, she's so very good to me. She don't often beat me;.. She's very

A Victorian portrait of a watercress seller. Often such portraits were not very realistic.

poor, and goes out cleaning rooms sometimes.

'I am a capital hand at bargaining . . . They can't take me in. For a penny I ought to have a full market hand, or as much as I could carry in my arms at one time, without spilling. For 3d. I has a lapful, enough to earn about a shilling; and for 6d. I gets as many crams my basket. I can't read or write, but I knows how many pennies goes to a shilling . . . When I've bought 3d. of creases, I ties 'em up into as many little bundles as I can. They must look biggish, or people won't buy them, so I puffs them out as much as they'll go . . .'

Further reading: *Mayhew's Characters* edited by P. Quennell (Spring Books, 1979), from a selection taken from *London Labour and the London Poor* by Henry Mayhew.

3

Early Careers for Middle-Class Women

c. 1840–1900

While working-class women faced the restrictions of protective legislation and tried to combine family life with a working life, some middle-class women in the nineteenth century began to try to re-establish the 'right to work'.

If the wife or daughter from a comfortably off background took up paid employment, she was thought to be advertising the fact that her father or husband was not rich enough to be able to pay for all her needs himself. As a young girl, the career she aimed at and was 'educated' for was marriage, and her 'work' was making herself accomplished enough to attract a wealthy husband.

However, by 1851 there were half a million more women in Britain than men. Thousands of women, therefore, could not marry, and had to try to support themselves. A middle- or upper-class woman who had to earn her own living and yet remain respectable and 'ladylike' had very few options open to her. Most women in this position tried to get work in another rich household, perhaps as a companion to an elderly or invalid lady, or more usually as a governess to teach the family's children. This became a very overcrowded occupation, as well as being badly paid and lonely. Although the governess had usually come from a comfortable background, she did not really belong socially either with the family who employed her, or with the rest of the servants, who often saw her as a 'cut above' them. In 1843, the Governesses' Benevolent Association was formed to help the many women who had at one time worked as governesses, and had later become destitute through illness or old age.

Many governesses and teachers in private day or boarding schools for the daughters of the wealthy, were not able to provide a very good education for their pupils because they themselves knew so little. Mathematics, especially, was a subject of which many girls from wealthy homes knew almost nothing. Without access to better education themselves, women's career prospects could never improve. In 1848, Queen's College was opened in London, followed in 1849 by Bedford College. These schools were mainly for young women, from twelve years of age, who wanted

Above A famous drawing by the Victorian artist Richard Redgrave of a young, unhappy governess. A middle-class woman who had to support herself had very few options, apart from work as a governess or milliner.

'
The definition of a governess, in the English sense, is a being who is equal in birth, manners, and education, but inferior in worldly wealth. . . Quarterly Review, Vol. 84
'

'
Miss Buss stated that girls left school with only such education as was almost entirely showy and superficial; a little French . . . but comparatively no knowledge of English and arithmatic . . .
Parliamentary Papers, 1867–68.
'

Below 1870: Elizabeth Garrett at her examination in Paris to become a doctor. Women were barred from being registered as doctors in Britain until 1877.

Right A romanticized view of Florence Nightingale's work during the Crimean War, which improved the image of nursing, gradually making it a more accepted career for middle-class women.

to be governesses. The first classes covered academic subjects such as mathematics, which had been virtually unavailable to women before. More advanced lectures were later introduced, in more unusual subjects for women, such as science.

Several of the students at these colleges later became very well known. Among them were the writer George Eliot, one of the first women doctors, Sophia Jex-Blake, and the founder of the famous North London Collegiate College, Frances Buss.

Freedom to be able to go on to university education was essential for women who wanted to qualify as doctors. But women were barred from becoming registered as doctors in Britain until 1877. Sophia Jex-Blake, who was enrolled at the Medical School of Edinburgh University, fought hard for ten years to achieve her ambition. Before this, only two other women had practised medicine in Britain. They were Elizabeth Blackwell and Elizabeth Garrett, who had both become registered as doctors abroad. Once women had won the right to work as doctors on the same terms as men, the number of women doctors in Britain increased rapidly, and by 1920 there were over 2,000.

Throughout the nineteenth century women had been able to work in hospitals as nurses, but nursing did not become a 'respectable' profession until Florence Nightingale's much praised achievements in the Crimean War (1853–56), and her opening of a training school for nurses at St. Thomas' Hospital in London. Along with elementary school teaching, nursing came to be thought of as a desirable profession for working-class girls who wanted to 'rise above their station', and middle-class girls who needed to earn their own living. Shop work also provided a respectable 'living-in' career for girls, so long as they did not mind the long hours and strict rules that generally went with it.

From the 1850s onwards, a determined effort was made to improve

employment prospects for middle-class women. The 'Society for Promoting the Employment of Women' was founded in 1859. Jessie Boucherett, Bessie Rayner-Parkes, Barbara Boudichon, Adelaide Anne Procter and Sarah Lewin all helped to organize the society. They were keen to convince people that training for a job and being at work did not make a woman any less 'feminine'. The kind of work the society suggested for educated women usually had a 'craft' or 'artistic' bias. Some examples were: shoe-making, wood engraving, interior design and hairdressing, all of which were previously almost totally dominated by men.

When it became clear that employment prospects for middle-class girls in offices, banks and shops would improve if their knowledge of figures was greater, Jessie Boucherett organized very popular training sessions in book-keeping. The society also set up a printing enterprise and encouraged women to train as printers and compositors.

By the end of the nineteenth century increased use of type-writers and telephones widened job prospects for women and, as business and industry expanded, there was also a greater need for clerical and administrative workers. The Civil Service was also beginning to provide new job opportunities for women, usually on lower rates of pay than men. Women worked in government offices as clerks, post office sorters, telegraph and telephone operators. Like teachers and nurses, women who worked for the Civil Service acquired training, job security and a pension; hours of work were also shorter than those of most other working women.

Secretarial work began to be seen as a job which was especially suitable for women, as it required neatness, care, obedience, dedication and subservience to the (usually male) employer.

Above By the end of the nineteenth century, as businesses expanded in cities, there was a growing need for women to do clerical work.

6

Miss Minnie Moore ... has at present only a small room ..., but it is nicely fitted up, is very clean indeed, and contains all that is essential to the comfort of ladies, for either shampooing, cutting or dressing of hair... The Englishwoman's Review, 1876.

9

6

In the morning, at nightfall and in the luncheon hour women pour in and out of every block of office buildings in numbers that rival the men ... The city is no longer man's domain ... M. Mostyn Bird, Women at Work, 1911.

9

Above 1832: A cartoon by George Cruickshank called 'Factory Slaves'. During the nineteenth century women became involved in the trade union movement to try and improve working conditions.

❛

Mary Leicster ... appearing in court ... having been ... tried and convicted at this session of a misdemeanour for that she and several other persons ... entered the mill, unlawfully, riotously and attacked and broke ... twenty engines ... the property of Richard Arkwright. Lancashire Records Office, 1780.

❜

❛

Miss Ruthwell, treasurer of the Power Loom Weavers' Society warned employers 'that the day was fast approaching when the tyranny practised on them [the workers] would end forever ...' and that workers would 'onward march to a fair day's wage for a fair day's work'. Northern Star, 1845.

❜

4

Women and the Labour Movement

c. 1830–1914

As middle-class women were working to establish careers for themselves, working-class women were trying to gain better conditions at work and fairer treatment. Trade unions, or 'combinations' of workers, were banned between 1799 and 1824. This period coincided with the growth of women's employment in industry. Employers took on female and child labour in preference to men to carry out the large numbers of jobs which demanded little training, and the idea that women's and children's work was worth lower wages than men's became well established. Factory owners seemed to prefer 'female hands' to work their machines, because they felt that women were less likely to cause trouble than male workers, who might try to 'combine' and act together to demand better wages or working conditions.

However, some women workers did take action against their employers. Even at the beginning of the Industrial Revolution women were involved with a group called the Luddites, who attacked the new spinning machinery which was threatening their jobs.

When trade unions were able to operate legally again from 1824, women found that they were not welcomed by, as well as usually being unqualified for membership of, some unions set up by skilled and better-paid male workers. Many male trade unionists saw women as a threat, a part of the labour force which could be used by the bosses, as and when it suited them, to work for lower wages and so undermine wage rates which the men's unions had struggled to obtain.

In some places there were exceptions. The cotton industry unions accepted women as members on the same terms as men; and Lancashire women had a strong tradition of trade union organization and political struggle. In the main, however, women generally remained outside the organized trade union movement until the last quarter of the nineteenth century.

Some working women did become very much involved in the Owenite Socialist movement, founded on the ideas of Robert Owen. The movement viewed women as equals to men and believed in the sharing of wealth, rather than ruthless competition and selfishness. Many women from a variety of trades joined Robert Owen's Grand National Consolidated Trade Union when it was formed in 1834, including 1,000 women stocking makers in Leicester. Women were also involved in the forming of the 'Society of Industrious Females' in 1832.

The greatest working-class movement of the first part of the nineteenth century was Chartism. This was based on the People's Charter, which demanded parliamentary reform, including votes for all men over twenty-one. Women workers joined Chartist groups throughout the country, and took part in meetings and demonstrations – even making speeches, although this was likely to earn them disapproval.

As the nineteenth century progressed, many trade unionists became unhappy about their wives and daughters having to go out to work. The idea began to grow that a married woman, especially if she had children, should stay at home to run the house and let her husband earn a 'family' wage. This assumed that all

Above An early trade union card of 1832, belonging to a woman member of the Power Loom Weavers' Society.

THE WIFE AT HOME.

"Oh, Jane, Jane!" exclaimed a mother, who was the wife of a working-man, as she stood at a neighbour's door, "you know I was out 'charring' yesterday, and earned a shilling, which was a little help to my husband's wages, but what do you think! while I was out, some of the children broke my new eightpenny pitcher, and then they either swallowed or melted nearly a whole quarter of a pound of butter, and I had nothing but dry bread for my supper!"

"Well, now," replied her neighbour (who was one of the wise mothers who would *not* go out to work), "I am truly sorry — your shilling *is more than lost*. It has long been my opinion, and here is a proof of it, that *a wife and mother should be a keeper at home.*"

> 6
> *The most respectable portion of the carpenters and joiners 'will not allow' their wives to do any work than attend to their domestic and family duties.*
> The Morning Chronicle, 1850.
> 9

Left This newspaper article of 1864 tried to discourage mothers from working. Few women had a choice – they worked to eat and clothe themselves and their family.

'■■■■■■■■

I joined the Felt Hatters Trade Union . . . Then we began to try and get the other girls in. It was hard work, the answer would be 'I will when the others do'. . . behold, when we got a majority . . . the master locked us out for six weeks. Mrs J.P. Scott in *A Felt Hat Worker.*

■■■■■■■■■ '

Above A woman chainmaker at Cradley Heath, the Midlands, in 1899. The Women's Trade Union League defended women's right to work in such jobs.

women *did* have husbands, who earned enough and were willing to support a wife and children.

In 1874, Emma Patterson founded the Women's Protective and Provident League (later known as the Women's Trade Union League,WTUL) and with a small group of middle-class women encouraged and helped to fund small trade unions for women in several occupations such as dressmaking, upholstering, printing and bookbinding. None of these unions survived for long, but the pressure exerted by Emma Patterson from 1875 onwards, as the first woman delegate to the Trades Union Congress (TUC), established the principle that women had a right to participate in the 'official' trade union movement.

In 1887, Clementina Black of the WTUL proposed at the TUC that 'where women do the same work as men, they shall receive equal pay'. The League defended the right of women to work in heavy, 'unwomanly' trades such as chainmaking. Attempts by some male trade unionists in 1886–7 to prevent women working at the pit brows of coal-mines were unsuccessful, and a deputation of twenty-two 'pit-brow lassies', some in their working clothes, marched through central London to put their case to the government.

Women workers took the lead in the 'New Unionism' of the 1880s, when thousands of the lowest paid and unskilled workers organized themselves into trade unions for the first time. In 1888, women working for the match manufacturers Bryant and May in East London came out on strike after the socialist Annie Besant had drawn attention to the low pay and health hazards of their work, comparing these with the high profits of the company. Match workers were at risk from 'phossy jaw' – a cancer caused by the phosphorus they handled – and their backs were damaged and hair rubbed off by carrying heavy boxes on their heads at work. Supported by the WTUL and the London Trades Council, the matchgirls managed to win their dispute, and set up their own Matchmakers' Union – the largest union composed entirely of women and girls in England.

Other groups of women throughout the country, jute workers, laundresses and cigar makers, also took action at this time to try to improve their wages and conditions. Sometimes these workers were encouraged and helped by middle-class women sympathizers. The first women factory inspectors for 'women's trades' were appointed in 1893. By the 1890s, the WTUL was encouraging women workers to join trade unions by sending full-time women organizers to distribute leaflets and hold meetings and discussions in areas where there were large numbers of women workers not in trade unions.

Left An artist's impression of a procession during the famous matchgirls' strike of 1888.

6

Bryant and May, now a limited liability company, paid last year a dividend of 23 per cent to its shareholders ... Let us see how the money is made with which these monstrous dividends are paid... The hour for commencing work [for the matchgirls] is 6.30 am in summer ... and concludes at 6 pm. This long day of work is performed by young girls who have to stand the whole time. A typical case is that of a girl of 16 ... she earns 4s. [20p] a week.
Annie Besant, 'White Slavery in London', an article in *The Link* magazine, 1888.

9

6

The greatest gain was in 'the sense of self-reliance, solidarity and comradeship ... making certain that, whatever the difficulties and dangers of the future, they will never again be, like those of the past, without hope. Women's Trade Union Review, 1911.

9

In 1906 Mary Macarthur, an important figure in women's trade unions, founded the National Federation of Women Workers (NFWW). She publicized the bad working conditions of women workers, especially those in 'sweated' trades such as needlework, and home workers. During 1911, strikes hit many industries throughout Britain. The long hot summer of that year saw a spontaneous outburst of industrial action by badly paid women workers from the stifling, crowded factories of London's East End, beginning in the Millwall Food Preserving factory. A story went round that a mysterious, nameless, 'fat woman' had appeared in many factories, threatened the bosses, and led the women out on strike. This legendary figure was never found, but the women had plenty of reasons anyway for taking action: they were very badly paid (7 s. [35p] a week on average for women, and 3 s. [15p] for girls) and, as a result of the strikes, they eventually gained wage rises of 1–4 s. (5p–20p) a week. These strikes were especially remarkable because they started so suddenly, and spread so quickly, and because of the enthusiasm and self-confidence of the women who took part in them.

By the eve of the First World War, women had shown that they were a significant force in the labour movement, even though they were still not allowed to join many of the most powerful male trade unions (such as the engineers). However, equal pay and equal treatment with male workers remained a long way off.

Mary Macarthur (1880–1920)

Mary Macarthur was born in Glasgow. Her father, a staunch Conservative, owned a successful drapery business. She began her working life as a book-keeper in her father's firm. As a hobby, she wrote articles for a local Conservative newspaper, and in 1901 went to a meeting organized by the Shop Assistants' Union (SAU), intending to write a sarcastic account, making fun of trade unionism. However, the meeting convinced her of the vital importance of trade unions and proved to be a turning point in her life.

In two years she was president of the entire Scottish section of the union and the first woman on the SAU National Executive Committee. She moved to London in 1903 to become secretary of the Women's Trade Union League.

Mary Macarthur was very efficient and energetic. Her reputation as a powerful and inspiring public speaker, whether at formal conferences or at street corner meetings, gained many recruits. She would explain:

> A union is like a bundle of sticks. The workers are bound together and have the strength of unity . . . They have the power of resistance . . . A worker who is not in a union is like a single stick. She can easily be broken . . . An employer can do without one worker. He cannot do without all his workers.

In 1906, she launched the National Federation of Women Workers (NFWW) with herself as secretary. This organization, which soon had its own newspaper, *The Woman Worker*, had over 2,000 members and 17 branches, and was to act as a general union for all women workers.

Many women workers at this time were

Mary Macarthur. In 1906, she helped found the National Federation of Women Workers.

employed in 'sweated trades', that is, they were working at home or in small workshops for very long hours and low wages. Mary Macarthur staged an exhibition in 1906 which drew attention to the plight of these workers and set up the Anti-Sweating League to campaign on their behalf. As a result, in 1906 the government established Wages Boards; their task was to ensure minimum wage rates.

Throughout the First World War, she pressed for improvements in the wages and conditions of women workers, and together with the NFWW, whose membership rose from 11,000 in 1914 to 60,000 in 1919, did her best to ensure that women who replaced male workers should be paid at the 'men's rate'.

In 1919, Mary Macarthur went to Washington, USA, as an adviser to the International Labour Organization. She died tragically young in 1920.

Further reading: *Mary Macarthur - A Biographical Sketch,* Mary Hamilton, 1925.

5

In Service

c. 1880–1930

Throughout the nineteenth century and during the first half of the twentieth centuries, more women worked as servants than in any other job. For many families in cramped overcrowded homes it was a great advantage if daughters took up a 'living-in' job as soon as they were old enough. Many girls found it very lonely and miserable, as going into domestic service meant moving away from home to live among strangers who were not always kind or considerate.

In large establishments, all the servants had a rigidly defined position in the household, from the housekeeper, butler and cook, right down to the youngest scullery maid and between-maid, often called a 'tweeny'. Only the very rich could afford to employ many servants; middle-class families during the nineteenth century would have had perhaps half a dozen or fewer permanent staff. Less well-off families might only have employed one general servant. By the end of the nineteenth century there were fewer male servants, and domestic service was viewed as far more of a 'woman's job'.

Above In the late nineteenth and early twentieth century many thousands of working-class women became domestic servants.

Below 1900: domestic service was generally seen as 'women's work'. In this picture two parlour maids lay a table for lunch.

A between-maid's lot was the most unhappy one in any household. You had to serve two masters, the cook and the housemaid. You were at the beck and call of either and if you were working for one, the other would be screaming out for you to work for her. Margaret Powell, *My Mother and I,* 1972.

Above The laundry at Petworth House, Sussex in 1890, provided jobs for several female servants.

... The interview with the lady of the house ... was even more intimidating than the house itself. When I told her my name was Margaret Langley I could see she considered it a highly unsuitable name for a kitchen maid. .. she thought it should have been Elsie Smith or Mary Jones. Margaret Powell, *Below Stairs,* 1968.

Although it was fashionable throughout the nineteenth century for upper-class women to appear fragile and delicate, women working as servants were always assumed to be capable of doing heavy and unpleasant tasks. Carrying large jugs of hot water up several flights of stairs to the family's bedrooms each morning was the housemaid's job in the days before many houses had bathrooms. Heavy coal scuttles were hauled up and down stairs, as all heating was by coal fires which had to be cleaned and made up daily. Floors had to be scrubbed, and carpets, furniture, cutlery, kitchenware, ornaments and many brass fittings inside and outside the house were all cleaned frequently – by hand.

Servants had to get up between 5am and 6am and were at work almost continuously until 10pm or 11pm at night. Off-duty time was perhaps one half-day a week and a few hours on Sunday. Employers often expressed great concern about the religious and moral welfare of their servants, especially the female ones. Servant girls were discouraged from being 'flighty' and from having boyfriends. A girl who was found to be pregnant was sacked, with little hope of getting another job in service.

If a servant wanted to move to another job, a good reference or 'character' from their previous employer was essential. Wages and hours of work varied. In 1923 Daisy Noakes, a domestic servant in Brighton (see case study), earned £14 per year, with a 2s. 6d. (25p) rise at the end of her first year. Servants did not have any legal protection. Only a few employers would support their servants during periods of sickness, and the nature of the job made it hard to set up a union. When a Servants' Union was begun in 1890, it proved very difficult to keep it going and it did not last long.

Servants were expected to know their place. They had to wear a uniform, which was usually paid for by themselves or their family. Employers would often give their servant a new name if they thought their real name was unsuitable!

Why was it that so many women took up this kind of work? Domestic service was seen by people as more suitable for young girls than factory work for example, because women servants were far more 'protected' and 'controlled' than they would be in other kinds of jobs. It was just this lack of independence (along with low pay and long hours) that made domestic work so unpopular, but for many women there was little alternative.

After the First World War there was much discussion about 'the servant problem' when richer people found that women who had done other jobs during the war did not want to go into service again. Later on in the 1930s, as jobs became scarce, many women did return unwillingly to domestic service.

Daisy Noakes (b. 1908)

Daisy Noakes was born and brought up in Brighton, the sixth of ten children. Her father worked as a milkman, and later in a local factory. Daisy started her first job 'in service' in December 1922 at the age of fourteen. In her autobiography *The Town Beehive*, she gives a picture of her childhood, and the years she spent as a servant before her marriage in 1934. The book describes how, by the time she was old enough to go out to work, she had already had plenty of experience of household chores. Two of her older sisters were also servants, and one of them 'spoke for' (recommended) Daisy to her own employers – the owners of a private school. Daisy got the job, at a wage of £14 for the first year, with the promise of a rise after that. Before starting work all her savings from holiday and after-school jobs were spent on buying material from which her mother made her uniform: 'Mum made me two blue dresses for morning wear,

half-lined, one black dress for afternoon wear, and four large bibbed white aprons. I had two caps for morning wear, frill caps for afternoons were supplied, one pair of ward shoes for mornings, one pair high-lows for afternoons and three pairs of black stockings . . . '

She goes on to describe her working hours: 'My hours were from 5.30 am to 10.30 pm and no let-up anywhere during that time. How I stayed awake I do not know. My off-duty time was Tuesday 2.30 pm to 9.30 pm, and one afternoon a fortnight for the same hours.' Getting back late from 'time-off' was treated as a serious matter. One evening Daisy got in late, and was caught by the under-matron. 'She was absolutely livid . . . and said she was reporting us to the matron in the morning, and it would probably mean the sack. I trembled as I stood there . . . not because of her, but one could not get a job without references, and I knew I could not go home.'

As third dormitory maid, Daisy Noakes came well below the parlour maid and pantry maid in status, but above the 'tweeny' or between-maid. Later on, she was promoted to parlour maid, a job which she liked very much, even though she once nearly lost it by sliding down the bannisters and crashing into the butler who was carrying a tray of glasses.

Summing up her early years and her job as a servant, she wrote: 'I would not wish any daughter of mine to work as hard as I had to as a child. But it was accepted, because it was the only job for girls, apart from shop assistants. . . '

Daisy Noakes (standing behind the young girl) with other domestic servants.

Extracts from *The Town Beehive – A young girl's lot (Brighton 1910–1934)*, Daisy Noakes (QueenSpark Books, 1978)
Further reading: *Faded Rainbow*, Daisy Noakes (QueenSpark Books, 1980).

Above *Women workers made a tremendous contribution to the war effort during the First World War.*

'———
I was in domestic service and hated every minute of it when war broke out, earning £2 a month working from 6.00am to 9.00pm. So when the need came for women 'war workers' my chance came to 'out'. Letter from Mrs H.A. Felstead, quoted in *Women at War* (1914–18).
———,

'———
... Engineering's not suitable work for women ... Oh yes, of course ... very clever with their fingers, no doubt, but it's not women's work. Quote from a Ministry of Munitions official, April 1917.
———,

6

Women and War Work

1914–1918

The involvement of their country in the First World War (1914–1918) brought many women the experience of working in new types of jobs. At first the need to equip Britain's armed forces led to more work becoming available in industries where women already 'traditionally' worked, such as tailoring (to provide all the extra uniforms), and leather and footwear manufacture (for boots, belts, equipment for horses and so on). David Lloyd George, as Minister of Munitions in the government which took office in 1915, called for women to register for war work at their local labour exchanges and thousands did so.

By the middle of 1915, women workers began to appear in different kinds of jobs, many of which brought them into contact with the public for the first time, as bank and post office clerks, ticket collectors, window cleaners. There was no government plan for women to do such work; in many cases women just took over from their husbands, fathers or brothers who had gone to fight. People found it hard to get used to the idea of women doing what had always been thought of as men's jobs, so replacement workers were sometimes given special names – garage attendants were known as 'petrol nymphs' and road sweepers were called 'street housemaids'.

At first there was considerable opposition to the idea of women working in munitions (weapons) and engineering factories on the same basis as men. As the war went on, however, it became obvious that unskilled women workers would *have* to be employed, if enough weapons, shells and ammunition were to be made. Generals said that they could do much better in battle if only they had more shells to fire at the enemy. After conscription was introduced in 1916, the need for women to take the place of men at work became even more urgent.

Very few 'munitionettes', as they were called, received sufficient training to do the most highly skilled jobs as precision engineers. Most factory managers assumed that women preferred simple repetitive jobs and were not really capable of anything more demanding.

Left *During the First World War women carried out jobs previously thought of as only being suitable for men. These women are working as railway porters.*

Semi-skilled or unskilled women were allowed to 'substitute' for skilled men workers only as a temporary emergency measure until the war ended, so that the wages and conditions negotiated before the war by the unions for their male members would not be harmed. Skilled women who 'substituted' for the skilled male workforce earned lower wages than the men, and worked very long hours.

The government and the media liked to think that women of all classes and all walks of life were joining together to help win the war. In fact, very few middle-class women worked in the munitions factories. With overtime (which was often compulsory), munitions girls could make £3 to £5 per week. Before 1914, the average weekly wage for an unskilled woman industrial worker was 11 s. 7 d. (approximately 58p), and many earned less. Even though their pay was much lower than the men's, girls working during the war had never before been able to earn so much money doing factory work.

Women in munitions factories ran a high risk of illness or injury

'
We put the brains into the machines before the women begin, explains the manager of a successful shell factory . . . From Barbara Drake's *Women in the Engineering Trades,* 1917.
'

'
At one London factory, protected by the Munitions Act, overtime was compulsory and paid at mere time rates. On each shift of thirty girls, six would take turns to go outside . . . to recover from the fumes. From Ross Davies' *Women and Work,* 1975.
'

Above Women working in an aircraft factory in early 1918.

> *In Leeds, a sixteen-year-old girl armaments worker was hurt in her machine after a 25 ½ hour shift ... A magistrate dismissed her case saying 'The most important thing in the world today is that ammunitions shall be made'.* From Ross Davies' *Women and Work*, 1975.

> *In 1917 at the age of 19, I joined the VADs ... in Boulogne ... we had to go at night with the drivers to meet the trains bringing the wounded, and the next morning at 11.00am two of us would attend the burials – I can never forget those lines of coffins ...* Letter from Miss Violet Flemming Frend about her experiences in the First World War.

because of their work. A free daily pint of milk was allowed to those working with TNT, but other safety precautions were not always put into practice. Women who handled TNT were sometimes called 'canary girls' because their skin changed to a bright yellow colour. The health risks from other dangerous substances, such as copper dust and aircraft varnish, were often played down because of the urgent need for weapons. Over 70 women workers were killed and many more were injured as a result of factory explosions during the war.

Women not only participated in the First World War as workers on the 'home front'. Some had jobs which took them much closer to the actual fighting as members of one of the Women's Auxiliary sections of the army, navy or airforce. At the beginning of the war some women travelled abroad to work – unpaid – as nurses helping to care for sick and wounded troops. Women who joined the Volunteer Aid Detachments (or VADs as they were called) came from rich enough backgrounds not to need any wages. Members of the First Aid Nursing Yeomanry (FANY) – founded in 1907 – also had to be wealthy enough to provide their own horses. However, as the war progressed, more nurses were desperately needed, so the War Office decided that VADs would have to be paid, to encourage more recruits. By 1916, 10,000 new VADs had joined the war effort, and many were young working-class women.

It was not until the spring of 1917 that the Women's Army Auxiliary Corps (WAAC) was set up. It was only after women had shown themselves able to do 'men's' work on the home front, that the army high command began to take the idea of the WAAC seriously. There were four different kinds of work in the WAAC – office work, cooking, mechanical and miscellaneous – all of which took place behind the front lines, freeing more men for fighting.

The WAAC was quickly followed by the formation of the Women's Royal Naval Service (WRNS) and the Women's Royal Auxiliary Airforce. Women in all the uniformed services did not receive the same wages as their male counterparts, and were not considered capable of the same work as men. For example, four 'technical women' or four 'women clerks' were thought to be able to do the same work as three 'technical soldiers' or 'soldier clerks'. Women doctors in the WAAC had to work for lower wages than the army's male medical officers – even lower than they could earn in civilian life.

The Women's Land Army came into being in 1917. This nationwide organization provided help for farmers whose male workers had gone into the army. They helped to try and increase the country's production of food supplies, especially after food rationing was introduced. By 1918, there were about 113,000 women working on the land. Like some munitions workers, women Land Army workers wore trousers, and this aroused fears that they might not behave in a very 'ladylike' way.

Despite the many disadvantages and hardships of their war-time jobs, many women looked back on their experience of war work as a time when they tasted independence and freedom. They felt the old view that women should stay at home and keep quiet could never be quite as powerful again.

> **'** *You are doing a man's work and so you're dressed rather like a man, but remember just because you wear a smock and breeches you should take care to behave like a British girl who expects chivalry and respect from everyone she meets.* Extract from the *Women's Land Army Handbook.* **'**

> **'** *The nation's debt to these women, many of whom lost their husbands in the war, is so great that it may even be likened to the debt which the nation owes to its soldiers and seamen.* From 'Our Amazons', an article in the *Daily Chronicle,* 1918. **'**

Left *Often the jobs undertaken by women involved heavy, physical work. Women wore trousers because they were practical, although some people felt they made women appear 'unfeminine'.*

Above 1932: *Women workers from Lancashire arrive in London after their three-week 'hunger march' to protest against the hardships and unemployment brought about by the Depression.*

7

Between the Wars

1919–1939

As the soldiers came back at the end of the war, women still at work were pressurized to hand in their notice, so that their jobs could go to the men. Women workers who lost their jobs in 1918 and 1919, and who applied at labour exchanges for unemployment benefit were told that they should return home, or to their former 'women's work' as servants, dressmakers, laundry maids and so on.

However, by the time the war ended, many women felt they had proved throughout the war years their ability to do work which had previously been thought of as only suitable for men. They were confident that they would now be accepted as having an equal value to that of men, both as workers and as useful members of society.

For a short while, politicians seemed to go along with this attitude. In Britain, women over the age of thirty gained the right to vote for the first time; this is often regarded as a 'reward' for their wartime work. The Sex Disqualification (Removal) Act became law in 1919. This said that no one could now stop women from working as lawyers, or in government jobs, and they were not to be sacked if they married. There was even a section agreeing to the principle of equal pay for women workers in the Treaty of Versailles, which the British government signed in 1919.

But this recognition of equality did not last for long, and did not get rid of all the unequal treatment women had to face at work. Women workers were put at a disadvantage by a new international agreement, 'The Washington Convention', which stopped women (classed with children and young people) from working night shifts in industry. This meant that many of the better-paid jobs, for example in the printing trade, became closed to women, just as some work in the nineteenth century had been, on the grounds that it was for women's own protection. However, traditional women's work like nursing – where night work was involved, but where there was no competition with men for high wages – was not affected by these rules.

In 1921, the British economy hit a slump and unemployment

> **6**
>
> *A person shall not be disqualified by sex or marriage from . . . being appointed to or holding any civil or judicial office or post, or from entering or . . . carrying on any civil profession or vocation.*
> Opening words of first clause of the *Sex Disqualification (Removal) Act*, 1919.
> **,**

rose sharply. Almost all the gains women workers had achieved during and just after the war seemed to evaporate. Any idea of equal pay for equal work was forgotton by the government and employers, and women in many jobs, such as teaching or in the Civil Service, had to resign if their employer knew they had got married.

The parts of Britain which relied upon traditional 'heavy' industries (coal, iron, steel and shipbuilding) in areas such as Wales, south Liverpool, Sheffield, Glasgow and Newcastle, suffered greatly during the Depression throughout the 1920s and the first part of the 1930s. Mostly it was men who were out of work in these areas, but the textile industry, where many women worked, was also badly hit. In the South and South East, however, the Depression was less severe and here new 'light' industries grew up. Electrical goods and household gadgets, along with other luxury items such as records, make-up and radios, were made on production lines in the new factories by semi-skilled workers – often women.

Advertising and hire-purchase schemes persuaded better-off housewives that they could not do without labour-saving equipment such as vacuum cleaners. Certainly, some middle-class women had to concern themselves more with housework, as 'living-in' domestic servants became scarce during the early 1920s. As the Depression got worse, however, women were forced back into service so that there were 200,000 more female servants in 1931 than in 1921. Unemployed women who refused to take jobs as servants, even for the ridiculous wage of £1 a week, lost their right to unemployment pay.

The hardships of unemployment during the inter-war years gave rise to many demonstrations and hunger marches. Women took part in these alongside men, and in 1932 a three-week march from Lancashire to London included a separate women's contingent, drawn from all the big industrial towns of the north of England.

Some people suggested that women having jobs while men were out of work was one of the causes of unemployment, and that women did not really have any right to work at all. The issue of their 'right to work' had been affecting women's lives since the Industrial Revolution, and is still ever present as an issue today.

Despite the Depression, it gradually became less unusual in the years between the two world wars for those girls who were better off to take up a career after leaving school, rather than just waiting to get married. Commuting into London and other large cities to earn a salary as a secretary or a typist meant a chance for economic independence.

> ' *... It was when the Civil Service regulations came to be dealt with, that it began to dawn on a considerable section, that the Act [Sex Disqualification (Removal) Act] meant very little indeed ... Then the women teachers began to wonder: 'A person shall not be disqualified by sex or marriage' ... yet they continued, as before, to be dismissed on marriage.* Article in *Time and Tide* magazine, 1922. '

Joan drove a car for her living.

WOULD YOU LIKE TO BE A CHAUFFEUSE?

So many girls are motor-minded these days that they can drive cars as easily as their brothers. Whether you are inclined this way or not, you will be interested in

"JOAN IN SEARCH OF A JOB," the new series of complete tales beginning next week.

Above This illustrated magazine story of 1930 reads 'so many girls are motor-minded these days that they can drive cars as easily as their brothers'. Gradually women were becoming more accepted in such 'unusual' jobs.

Above 'Business girls' of the 1930s. More women were taking up a career after leaving school, rather than just waiting for marriage.

'

The pay . . . was 27s. 6d. [£1–35p] a week, but we had 'discrepancies' stopped from that, which often left me owing J. Lyons money . . . If we forgot to charge a customer for rolls and butter, or if someone stole them, we had to pay for this ourselves. Mrs L. Brown in *Where we used to Work.*

'

Although their salaries were usually quite meagre, some 'business girls' managed to live away from home in flats or bedsitters. If they could afford it, they went out to teashops, cocktail bars and the cinema; they wore make-up and copied the clothes and hairstyles of the latest glamorous film stars. In these respects, they felt themselves to have more freedom and control over their own lives than would have seemed possible to their mothers' generation.

Some women also found work in the new jobs connected with the growing 'leisure industries' of the 1920s and 1930s. Work as a waitress – for example as a 'Nippy' in one of Lyons Tea Shops – or as a cinema usherette, were alternatives to domestic service, factory, shop or office work for many girls, and although the pay tended to be low, tips provided a little extra money.

The 1921 Census showed that 86 per cent of all women professional workers were in teaching or nursing, traditional women's occupations without equal pay. A few women, however, were beginning to make their careers in other professions, for example as vets, barristers or architects, although they had to be prepared to fight against male prejudice. Some new careers, such as those concerned with scientific research, aviation and engineering, were also beginning to attract well-educated women.

8

Women in the Second World War

1939–1945

When Britain entered the Second World War in September 1939, no immediate plans existed for women to join in the war effort. Those who tried to get war jobs were often turned down, despite official pleas for more war workers. Some government propaganda said that the best contribution women could make to the war effort was on the 'kitchen front', staying at home cooking nutritious meals, not listening to rumours and generally keeping up family morale.

However, after the fall of France and the evacuation of British soldiers from Dunkirk in 1940, many civilians were called up. This left great gaps in the workforce at home, so the Minister of Labour, Ernest Bevin, called for at least 1.5 million women to volunteer for work. Too few women in fact responded, so war work soon became compulsory. The National Service (No.2) Act was passed in December 1941, conscripting all single women between the ages of eighteen and thirty, either into the armed forces or into industry.

Eventually all women, married and single, up to the age of 50 were registered for work. The rules about call-up did not apply to wives of men serving in any of the forces – but many of these women went into war work anyway. Britain was the first country involved in the Second World War to conscript women, and most women accepted the idea without much protest. By 1943, almost all women of working age (14–65) without dependent children were involved in some kind of essential job, or were in the forces.

The 10 million women with domestic responsibilities worked in auxiliary nursing, civil defence, or as members of the Women's Voluntary Service. Many of them combined several jobs, working full- or part-time in a factory or office, and doing voluntary work in their spare time as well. The 'official' attitude towards women workers still tended to be that they were troublesome and unreliable, both 'by nature' and because of the 'problem' of women's domestic responsibilities. Picking young children up from school and arranging care when they were ill did not fit in very easily with the way factory life was organized. There were virtually

Above Auxiliary Territorial Service (ATS) members during the Second World War.

> *... Now in this great crisis ... the Ministry of Food has no use for women except to tell each one in her own kitchen to make the best of short rations ...*
> From *Bombers and Mash: The Domestic Front 1939–45.*

> *It didn't seem to dawn on the government that any woman in war work really had two jobs, because she had to do her shopping ... and the shops were closed when you finished work.*
> Elaine Burton in *A People's War.*

Above A young woman trains for skilled engineering work. Factory safety was often very poor – this woman does not even have a mask to protect her eyes from the dangerous metal swarf.

' *I was fighting like mad with my parents to be allowed to go into the armed forces, because my brothers were all in it. The argument was, well, you're the girl, you should stay at home with mother.* Margaret Kippin in *What did you do in the War, Mum?* '

Right ATS members working with anti-aircraft equipment to spot enemy planes.

no women in senior government posts who might have been able to influence government policy to make life a little easier for working mothers.

Many women had to rely on neighbours or friends to look after their children. By 1944, 1,450 nurseries run by local authorities had been set up in Britain, in comparison to 104 which existed before the war. Nevertheless, the nursery places were still insufficient for the needs of 5.5 million working women.

Although they were earning good wages, especially compared with pre-war pay, most women factory workers were still earning very much below the rates paid to men. The question of equal pay for women was much discussed as the war continued. A survey in 1942 found that 95 per cent of women interviewed were in favour of equal pay, and there were several strikes and disputes about wage levels. More women joined trade unions during the war – some even managed to become members of the exclusive Amalgamated Engineering Union (AEU), who accepted its first women members in 1943.

Just as in the First World War, women also took over jobs previously thought of as men's work. They worked on railways as engineers, delivered milk and letters, repaired houses, fixed plumbing, worked as gas fitters and swept chimneys.

About two-thirds of women conscripted chose to join one of the armed forces instead of working in industry. The ATS (Auxiliary Territorial Service), the WAAF (Women's Auxiliary Air Force) and the WRNS (Women's Royal Naval Service) did not actually take part in active combat, but they were trained to do almost every other kind of work. After basic training, women in all three services could continue with courses to acquire more highly-paid

technical skills, for example in electrical and mechanical repair work, in the operation of radar and radio as well as code-breaking. Women drivers in the services were totally responsible for the maintenance and repair of their lorries, motorbikes and jeeps.

From 1940, the ATS worked alongside men in the operation of anti-aircraft guns. Members of the WAAF also controlled the huge barrage balloons which were launched to deter low-flying enemy bombers. Despite prejudice against them, women pilots flew training aircraft and delivered all the new planes to RAF bases.

By 1944, 80,000 women had joined the Women's Land Army (WLA) as volunteers or conscripts. Britain's food output became almost double what it was at the start of the war, and much of this could be credited to the WLA. 'Landgirls' wore distinctive uniforms, and either lived in hostels or were billetted with families. Their work was hard and dirty and they worked long hours. But, for many, the good company of the other landgirls and the benefits of living and working in the open air away from the crowded and bombed cities made up for all this.

Women also took a major role in dealing with the horrific effects of the massive air-raids on many British towns and cities. The 4.5 million Civil Defence Volunteers included many women, acting as air-raid wardens, firewomen, rescue workers, ambulance drivers, messengers and first-aiders. Women also ran the control centres which co-ordinated and directed the rescue services.

During the final months of the war, everyone looked forward to a return to pre-war 'normality'. Certainly many women felt by the end of the war that they needed a good long rest, but it is not so easy to discover if most really wanted to retreat permanently into their homes again.

In 1945, the Control of Employment Act meant that demobilized men had priority over women in signing on for jobs at the Labour Exchange. Although women were praised and thanked for having helped towards the final victory of the war, there were no 'rewards' for their contribution. Equal pay was much discussed, but was still unusual even in the engineering and munitions trades. Winston Churchill refused to allow women teachers equal pay with men as part of the 1944 Education Act. He called it 'impertinence', although the same act did at last permit women teachers to keep their jobs after marriage.

Apart from the high wages that some women were able to earn, and the lasting friendships made with other women working alongside them, the most enduring benefit women gained from their experience of working during the Second World War, was the knowledge that they *were* able to do work which, because they were female, no one before had believed they could tackle.

> *The men didn't mind us flying the Tiger Moths because it was terribly cold – there was no heating and an open top. No matter what you did to avoid it, your face froze. We were so thrilled to be doing it that the idea of the freezing cold didn't bother us.* Joan Hughes in *A People's War.*

Below *By the end of the war there were over 80,000 landgirls, who helped produce vital food supplies during wartime rationing.*

Perfect timing...

Clever girl! She certainly deserves her bouquet—*not that he couldn't do it himself!* It's all so simple with Mr. Therm's NEW Gas cookers. They've got *everything* to take the drudgery out of cooking—eye-level grills, temperature regulators, spacious ovens, control of the flame you can *see* and the *instant heat you need.* Easy to clean, lovely to look at—there's no guesswork with Mr.Therm's cookwork—*and that saves fuel, fuss and food!* See Mr. Therm's Variety Show of modern Gas cookers at your Gas Showrooms and all on the easiest possible terms—with no *purchase tax!*

Above This 1950s advertisement for a gas cooker encourages women once again to take up the role of obedient, caring housewife.

> **There is a strong case indeed for believing that prolonged separation of a child from his mother ... during the first five years of life stands foremost among the causes of delinquent character development.** John Bowlby, *Child Care and the Growth of Love*, 1953.

Right Many women were forced to give up the jobs they enjoyed during the war, as nursery schools and child care facilities, set up during the war, were closed down.

9

Back to 'Normal'

1950–1969

When peace returned in 1945 thousands of women left work and went back to their homes. Why was this? Many people expected things to be just the same as before the war, when it was considered undesirable for a married woman to go out to work unless the family was really down on its luck. There was also much concern that if women were encouraged to go on working outside the home, not enough babies would be born to help boost Britain's falling population figures.

The Beveridge Report of 1942, parts of which were called the 'Housewives Charter', and which became the basis of the post-war Welfare State, had emphasized the important role of women as housewives and mothers. Family Allowances (similar

to present-day Child Benefit) were introduced as a kind of 'payment' to mothers, and in the 1950s some influential writers on child-rearing seemed to be suggesting that the best thing a caring mother could do to make sure her baby grew up happy and well balanced was to stay at home. Links were made between working mothers and the growth of juvenile delinquency.

Meanwhile, the National Health Service and the Social Services of the new Welfare State gave women who did want or need to work many more opportunities in traditional female jobs, such as providing health care, helping people with problems (as social workers), as well as cleaning, catering and so on. In fact, the need for women to work in the Health Service was so great that some women were especially recruited from overseas, particularly from Commonwealth countries.

The 'baby boom' that occurred after the war led to a call for more teachers, and women who had previously given up teaching to have a family were encouraged to return to the classroom. Despite vigorous campaigning, however, it was not until 1955 that women teachers and civil servants succeeded in getting the government to agree to the principle of equal pay with men; even then, it was not until 1961 that they finally received it. Other women workers in many different industries had to wait for another fourteen years after that.

At the end of the war, when child-care facilities which had been set up to help working women with their domestic responsibilities were being dismantled, many women workers who gave their views to interviewers and researchers mentioned that they would welcome the chance to continue working, but on a part-time basis. Little effort was made initially to provide this, except in certain specific industries, such as textile manufacture, where women were encouraged to stay at work to help with the export drive.

Britain's economy gradually got back on its feet during the first few years of the 1950s, and unemployment fell. Businesses started to expand and employers looked around for new workers. Firms began to organize 'twilight' shifts in the evening, or shifts during school hours.

The number of women with paid jobs increased. In 1961, for the first time, there were more married than unmarried women workers. More and more women worked on production lines, turning out TV sets, washing machines, cosmetics, processed foods, vacuum cleaners, refrigerators, and dozens of other household gadgets, which they themselves were being encouraged to buy in order to keep up with the current media image of the ideal wife and mother, who kept her home neatly furnished and spotless, her family well fed and cared for, and

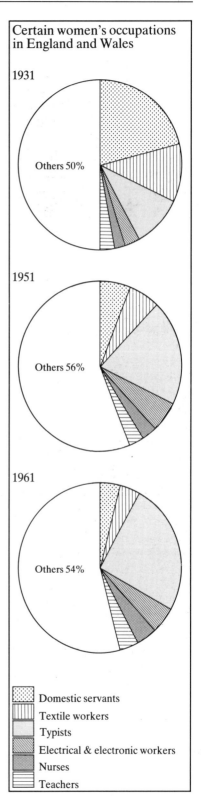

Certain women's occupations in England and Wales

1931 — Others 50%

1951 — Others 56%

1961 — Others 54%

Domestic servants
Textile workers
Typists
Electrical & electronic workers
Nurses
Teachers

herself always immaculately dressed and beautifully made up.

Apart from the important consideration of wanting company and an escape from the boredom of housework, women were said to be working in the 1960s to provide 'luxuries' for their families – like cars or foreign holidays. Certainly, such items came to be more within the reach of working-class families. However, on closer examination, the so-called 'extras' worked for by many women were in fact essential items, such as furniture, or clothes for the children. Despite this, the attitude that women only *needed* to work for 'pin money' helped to encourage the idea that it was still acceptable for women to work for lower wages than men.

Careers advice for girls still tended to assume that most women would just work at an uninspiring 'stop-gap' job for a few years before settling down to marriage and child care. Fewer girls than boys stayed on at school or went on to further education. Women made up only 27 per cent of the total number of higher education students in 1967–8 – the same proportion as in 1919–1920. Fewer women received proper job training in a skill which they could use to get a well-paid job, despite the fact that most women now had far smaller families, and after their youngest child had grown up they would still have at least fifteen to twenty years of working life ahead of them.

Women accounted for only 2 million out of the 10 million members of unions which belonged to the TUC by the end of the 1960s, although the numbers were steadily rising. The TUC launched its Women's Charter in 1963, which called for equal pay for work of equal value, and better working conditions and training facilities for all women workers. But, this had little effect – partly perhaps because the trade union movement itself was still dominated by men who did not always take women workers

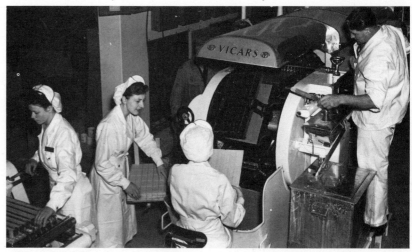

Right During the 1960s, there was a move towards married women taking up some form of part-time work. These women are working in a biscuit factory.

seriously. Nevertheless, 'official' attitudes *were* changing very gradually. The government's 'National Plan' of 1965 tried to discover if, and how, women workers could be used as a more effective and skilled part of the labour force.

Towards the end of the 1960s, the revival in Britain of the feminist movement (then known as 'women's liberation') coincided with the stepping up of calls for equal pay. In 1968, a group of women who worked at machining car upholstery in Ford's Dagenham factory came out on strike for three weeks to try to get more equal pay rates. This re-opened the old struggle. At the TUC conference of the same year, women delegates insisted that getting equal pay and equal rights for women's work should be one of the main goals of the trade union movement. In 1969, as a response to this growing campaign, and because equal pay was one of the rules of the Common Market, which Britain wanted to join, Barbara Castle, the Labour government's Minister of Employment, presented a Bill to Parliament giving warning that from 1975 it would become illegal for women in Britain not to receive the same wages as men doing the same work.

By the end of the 1960s, however, the position of women at work was perhaps not so different from what it had been earlier in the twentieth century. Women workers still tended to be concentrated in relatively few low-paid 'serving' or 'caring' occupations. But domestic service was no longer one of the chief areas of women's work; clerical, office and secretarial jobs had taken its place.

'Professional' or 'semi-professional' jobs done by women still tended to follow the old pattern. There were more women than men in education and medicine, but the women were almost always in the more 'lowly' jobs – working, for example, as nurses rather than doctors.

Part-time work, flexible hours or job sharing for professionally qualified women was almost non-existent, and regarded by many employers as inconvenient and unnecessary. It was generally still believed that women, especially those with families, were unlikely to 'get to the top', especially in traditionally 'male' professions, such as accountancy, architecture, banking or politics. True, women were now represented in almost all areas of work, but often only as isolated individuals. To make a success of an 'unusual' job, a woman had to be an 'unusual' person, able to face prejudice and criticism. Being competitive or ambitious was not really seen as a desirable character trait in women anyway. Even in the booming fashion and leisure industries of the 1960s, women who 'made it' to the top, like the designer Mary Quant, the model Twiggy or the singer Cilla Black, were few and far between.

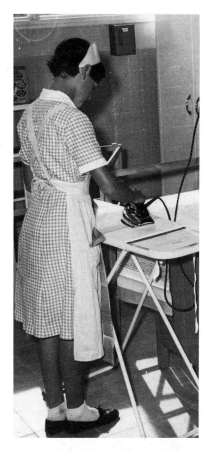

Above Some schools in the 1960s still taught girls housewifery.

> I gave up medical social work six weeks before the expected birth of my first son . . . like many other earnest mothers of the period I had read (and badly misconstrued) the work of John Bowlby. So I stayed at home to ensure the emotional well-being of my child, at great cost, at times, to my own.
> Sociologist quoted in Women at the Top, Achievement and Family Life, 1977.

Above By the 1970s more and more women were breaking into male-dominated professions, including Elizabeth Butler-Sloss, who became a High Court judge.

Below In the 1980s, the issue of equal pay for equal work continued.

10

Equal at Last?

1970–1979

New laws in the 1970s – the Equal Pay Act, the Sex Discrimination Act and the right to maternity leave – all seemed to promise many improvements for women at work. But as time went on it became clear that these new laws did not go anywhere near to giving women a guarantee that from now on they could be sure of completely equal and fair treatment.

Employers had five years to make preparations between the passing of the Equal Pay Act and the date on which it actually became law (29th December, 1975). The average pay for women workers rose, but when the law finally came into force, women were still only earning three-quarters of the average wage of men. This has continued to be the case since 1975.

Employers found it was quite easy to get round the wording of the Act, which was that women must receive equal pay if they were doing 'the same or broadly similar work as a man for the same employer at the same place of work'. If certain jobs in a particular workplace were only done by women (say filing in an office, for example), then the Act could not be used. Some areas of 'women only' work already existed, and employers set up many more. So long as there was no male worker doing the same job in the same place for more money than a woman, the Act did not apply. Between 1970 and 1975, many women also found that the kind of work they did was given a new title and grading, with perhaps some little details altered, making it legally not 'the same' work as that done by men working alongside them.

In 1975, another Act of Parliament, the Sex Discrimination Act, outlawed unfair treatment of women. Now it was not possible to refuse any job to a woman because, in her employer's opinion, it was 'unsuitable' to her sex. 'Indirect' discrimination against women looking for work was also covered by the Act. In 1977 a rule that some jobs in the Civil Service were not available to people over twenty-eight was found to be unlawful, because many women who had taken some years off work during their twenties to care for young children were less likely than men to be able to comply with this age limit.

A career in the London Fire Brigade
A future worth considering.

You may not previously have considered the possibility – but the London Fire Brigade represents a career challenge not just for men but for women too.

In providing its vital services to the most ethnically diverse capital city in the world, the London Fire Brigade can offer women and men of all races and from a wide variety of backgrounds a uniquely rewarding mix of job satisfaction, good pay, opportunities for promotion and long term prospects. Women, like all recruits, join as Firefighters, get the same chances to prove their ability and, if keen to do so, to make the most of their potential and go for promotion.

To become a London Firefighter you must live in Greater London, be 18-30 and physically fit, be at least 5'6" tall, have a 36" chest (with 2" expansion) and good unaided eyesight.

If you would like to find out more about a career with the London Fire Brigade send for further information now by returning the coupon to: London Fire Brigade, Room 506, Queensborough House, Albert Embankment, London SE1 7SD.

The GLC welcomes applicants from all sections of the community, irrespective of their sex, ethnic origin, colour, sexual orientation or disability, if they have the necessary attributes to do the job.

Under the terms of the Sex Discrimination Act it was now possible, in theory, for a woman to study, qualify and apply for any job she wished, although in practice it still took a lot of nerve to be the only girl in the motor mechanics class (or the only boy taking parentcraft); or the only woman lorry driver in the transport café.

Some job titles had to be changed to show that they were open to both sexes, for example 'fireman' was changed to 'firefighter'. Women who were beginning to take on 'unusual', formerly male, jobs were making front page news, but found that they still had to face hostility, ridicule or rudeness from the men they worked alongside.

Although the Sex Discrimination Act was an important step towards giving women more job choice, most working women continued to do the lower paid, boring or repetitive work which was still considered (although now perhaps not quite so openly), more 'suitable' for women.

The Employment Protection Act of 1976 included provision for maternity leave with some pay and gave mothers the legal right to return to work, if they wished, after having a baby. But this legislation only applied to women who had worked for at least two years full-time or five years part-time with the same employer, and so about half of all pregnant women working in Britain were not entitled to maternity leave. In fact it is still much more difficult to qualify for all the maternity provisions available by law in Britain than it is in any other European country.

The Equal Opportunities Commission (EOC) was set up by the government in 1975 to check that the Equal Pay and Sex Discrimination Acts were working properly, and to help people who wanted to use these Acts to try to get equal treatment. Based in Manchester, away from other government offices, the EOC has

Above With the passing of the Sex Discrimination Act in 1975, some job titles had to be changed. This advertisement encourages women to join the London Fire Brigade as firefighters.

'
I went round all the furniture workshops in Cambridge asking if they'd take me on as an apprentice; but they all refused. Some claimed they didn't have separate toilet facilities for women. Anna Cunningham, furniture restorer.
'

found it difficult to obtain more help for working women, for
example by providing more child care facilities, or better
conditions for part-time workers.

Around the same time as the new laws affecting women at work
were being put into practice, groups of women workers were
hitting the headlines by taking the lead in industrial disputes. In
the early 1970s, the women who cleaned office buildings at night
campaigned to improve wages and conditions and encouraged
night cleaners to join a trade union.

At Fakenham in Norfolk in 1972, some women took over and
ran their shoe factory to stop it from being closed down; the Trico
car component workers in Brentford, London, gained equal pay
in 1976 following a twenty-one week strike, despite an industrial
tribunal ruling that they were not entitled to it. Women at another
London factory, Grunwick, also took a leading part in a long
struggle (1976–78) for the right to join a trade union.

Some women trade union members issued a 'Working
Women's Charter', which combined 'traditional' demands for
better wages and shorter hours with those of the women's
liberation movement for such things as more nursery schools. By
1981 the TUC had established a policy of 'positive action', which
said that making laws was not enough on its own to ensure that
women gained equality at work, and that employers – and unions
– had to set up schemes to change sexist attitudes and assumptions
about women workers, and provide women with the chance to do
as well at work as men.

The problem of combining working hours with looking after a
home and children ceased to be seen as the sole concern of women.
Job sharing and 'flexitime' hours challenged the idea that a

*Right During the 1970s women were
very much involved in strike action to
gain better working conditions. In
1976, many employees at Grunwick's
photo-processing factory in North
London came out on strike for the right
to join a trade union.*

They're all happy with their choice!

Left In the 1970s and 1980s the Equal Opportunities Commission (EOC) produced a great deal of information for teenage girls choosing subject options at school. The pamphlet from which these pictures are taken is called 'A positive choice at 13 has a positive effect for life'. These girls are qualified (from left to right) as an electrician, a stonemason and a Merchant Navy officer.

'proper' job could only be undertaken within the traditional pattern of working hours. Women began to take themselves more seriously as workers with the right to a job or a career – on their own terms.

The hidden problem of sexual harassment at work, which had made many women's lives a misery, now began to be discussed and written about, and condemned as an unacceptable form of discrimination against women which could not be tolerated any longer.

By the early 1980s, magazine articles and books began to appear, giving women advice on how to 'get to the top' at work. Although the 'traditional' role of woman as housewife and mother was still very common, this was less often presented as the only 'real' career available, and it became acceptable for a woman to reject this role completely in favour of an ambitious career aim. 'Role reversal', with fathers staying at home to look after the house and children, while mothers became the family breadwinners, was still quite unusual, but not unknown, and less likely to earn disapproval or ridicule, especially from younger people. Some fathers as well as mothers began to plan their working lives around the wish to look after their children. Of course, with the economic recession of the 1980s, and rapidly growing unemployment, some families made such arrangements not out of principle, but from necessity.

With the election of Britain's first woman Prime Minister, Margaret Thatcher, in 1979, some people said that all the barriers to women's progress in any and every type of work had finally disappeared. However, although by the end of the decade women were far more visible members of the work-force, and the impact of the ideas of the women's movement was undeniable, the 1980s were to show that the disadvantages and difficulties many women had to put up with at work still existed.

'
1973: First women members of the London Stock Exchange.
1975: First women jockeys in Britain.
1975: First woman jet airline captain.
1976: First woman firefighter in Britain.
1976: First woman to serve as a British ambassador.
1976: First TV camerawoman.
,

'
I think too few fathers have a say in how their children are brought up . . . I feel I am being a proper father. . . Many of the women . . . say their husbands would love to do the same . . . the other reaction . . . is that I'm mad to be doing work that's beneath me – women's work. Steve Penneck, househusband and father, *Options* magazine, 1987.
,

Jayaben Desai

Jayaben Desai was born in Gujarat, India, but lived in Tanzania for many years. In 1969 she came to Britain, as many other East African Asian people were forced to do in the late 1960s and early 1970s.

Five years after her arrival, Desai began working full-time in the mail-order department of Grunwick's film processing factory in Willesden. Her son, Sunil, worked for the same firm. A large part of the workforce at Grunwick was female, and many of them were of Asian origin. Pay was low and the workers had many complaints, such as being forced to do compulsory overtime at very short notice, and having to ask permission to go to the toilet. Anyone who complained too much was given the sack, and there was no trade union at Grunwick to speak for the workers.

One Friday afternoon in 1976, after an argument with the managers about compulsory overtime, Jayaben and Sunil Desai walked out. Other workers at Grunwick soon joined in the dispute, especially after the company refused to recognize the right of employees to join a trade union.

During the course of the Grunwick strike, Jayaben Desai became a nationally known figure, as one of the leading members of the strike committee. At the start of the dispute, on the day she left Grunwick, Desai told the manager: 'What you are running here is not a factory, it is a zoo. But in a zoo there are many types of animals. Some are monkeys who dance on your finger tips, others are lions who can bite your head off. We are those lions, Mr Manager.'

Jayaben Desai and her fellow strikers did

Jayaben Desai – a leading figure in the Grunwick dispute.

not win the Grunwick dispute. After nearly two years, in July 1978, the strike was called off, without the owners of the firm having agreed to allow trade union membership among its workforce, even though a government inquiry led by Lord Scarman recommended that Grunwick should allow its workers to join a union if they wished.

Despite this eventual defeat, the dispute at Grunwick became an example for many people of how women workers, when they were pushed too far, were prepared to organize themselves to fight for basic rights and freedoms. Jayaben Desai's determined leadership made her one of the leading women in the British trade union movement during the 1970s.

Further reading: *Grunwick: The Worker's Story*, Jack Dromey and Graham Taylor (Lawrence and Wishart, 1978).

11

The 1980s Onwards

The severe economic recession of the early 1980s badly affected both men and women workers. However, fewer women than men lost their jobs overall. Most women in Britain were going out to work by the mid-1980s, and were likely to have a job for the major part of their adult lives. Although many women spent some time away from work when their children were born, the length of this 'baby break' gradually reduced. Also, very few women now give up work solely because of marriage.

A few firms now offer extra benefits to mothers over and above the legal minimum for maternity leave (which is twenty-nine weeks after the birth for an employee who has worked for the same company for two years). For example, they offer 'refresher'

Above By the 1980s women could be seen in many varied professions. This woman is a civil engineer on a construction site.

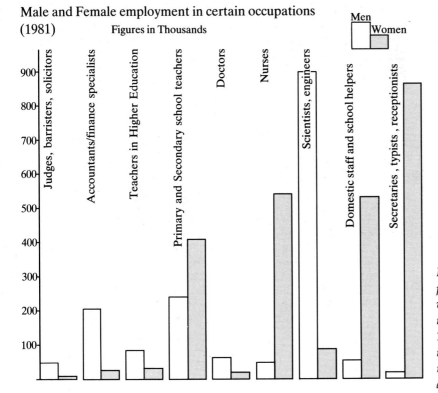

Male and Female employment in certain occupations (1981) Figures in Thousands

Men / Women

Left A bar graph showing the proportion of men and women in various occupations. Although great improvements had been achieved by 1981, women still tended to be found in jobs such as teaching and nursing, rather than accountancy, engineering and law.

Above In 1984, cook Julie Hayward took her employers, Cammel Laird, to court and won her case for equal pay for work of equal value.

Below Women account for only 0.5 per cent of the construction industry workforce.

courses for women who are returning to work after maternity leave, more flexible working hours, maybe even a workplace crèche. However, such firms are few and far between, and most women still find that little is done to encourage or assist mothers of young children to combine child care with work. Some employers still feel most girls do not want a career or even that they should be discouraged from competing with most men for promotion or training, on the grounds that sooner or later they are bound to have children, and it will all be 'wasted'.

A higher proportion of women with children under school age go out to work in some parts of Europe than in the U.K. The main reason for this seems to be the almost total lack of state child-care facilities in Britain (such as nurseries) and also after-school care for older children. Most working mothers in Britain are therefore forced to rely on private, often complicated, unreliable and expensive child-care arrangements, and few fathers are prepared or expected to sacrifice their career prospects, or to take primary responsibility for making suitable provision for child care.

Part-time work is overwhelmingly performed by women because they usually bear the responsibility of caring for children, and increasingly for older relatives as well. Thus, for mothers and other women who have unpaid work and responsibilities at home, a low-paid job but with part-time hours is highly sought after.

From school to training, young women are still generally encouraged into 'female occupations'. The Training Opportunities Programme (TOPS), run by the Manpower Services Commission (MSC), did little to challenge the traditional stereotypes of 'men's' and 'women's' work. Figures from 1980-81 showed that 97 per cent of those on shorthand and typing courses were women; along with 88 per cent of clerical students. In contrast, women only accounted for 0.5 per cent of the students taking courses in construction and welding, and for 1 per cent of those studying engineering and metal work.

In 1988, despite the efforts of various schemes such as GIST (Girls into Science and Technology) and WISE (Women into Science and Engineering), designed to encourage girls to train for work in areas connected with engineering, science, or technology, the number of girls actually taking up such careers was still very low. In fact, the total percentage of women in engineering (20 per cent) was 2 per cent *less* in 1988 than it had been for ten years previously. Most of those women (90 per cent of them in fact) were doing clerical or operative work. Only 4 per cent of all professional engineers and scientists were women.

The 'New Technology' of the 1980s has been responsible for the arrival of many new kinds of jobs, especially those involving

computing or microtechnology. However, the 'electronics revolution' has only created very limited opportunities for women to
take up more interesting, highly paid or skilled work. Despite the
fact that the first computer programmer was a woman (Ada
Lovelace, a nineteenth-century mathematician), women working
in computing by the early 1980s were to be found in few responsible or senior positions. In the USA the first operational computer
(the ENIAC), used during the Second World War, was pro-
grammed by a group of 100 women who were allocated the job
because it was seen as 'clerical' work, and therefore most suited
to 'female skills'. However, a survey carried out in 1986 showed
that only 18 per cent of programmers were women, even though
they accounted for 95 per cent of the total number of data prep-
aration workers.

Above The all-women company,
Microsyster provide advice for women on
careers in computing as well as being a
successful computer consultancy.

Below This woman executive is a
financial adviser for Sainsbury's
Supermarkets.

Nevertheless, the spread of new technology has resulted in
some benefits for women workers, and could potentially offer
many more. For example, the availability of more part-time and
flexitime work, as fast microtechnology reduces the number of
necessary working hours, has been seen as one development
which could make it possible for men to spend more time in
helping to run households and care for their families.

Taking on home-based or freelance data-processing work is

Above Women still continue their fight for better pay and working conditions. These nurses in 1988 are demonstrating about the lack of funds in the National Health Service.

Below Betsy Carroll – the first woman pilot to fly a Jumbo jet across the Atlantic, pictured at Gatwick airport.

another way in which it is possible for some women to organize working lives around their home commitments. One major company, F International, a highly successful firm providing data processing systems for many companies world-wide, was originally set up by a woman working from home.

Other women have also succeeded in setting up their own successful business enterprises. However, many women are still involved in areas which are 'traditionally female' – such as designing or beauty care. One such 'role model' was Anita Roddick, whose beauty products business developed into the Body Shop empire. Another, well established by the mid 1980s, was Laura Ashley, head of a world-wide fabrics, clothes and furnishings enterprise, which grew from humble origins in Wales.

The whole idea of the 'woman executive' has had great appeal, with continual promotions by the fashion industry of 'power dressing': for example clothes such as 'business suits', designed for the ambitious young woman, to give the right impression about her serious attitude to work. Articles in women's magazines designed specifically for the 'working woman' have given hints and advice on how to achieve success and get to the top. Books on the same theme are also popular. The contents of such publications often tend to encourage the idea that a working woman must aim to be a 'superwoman' – able to cope with all the responsibilities of a busy domestic and social life, as well as holding down a high-powered job. However, for the great majority of working women, such an image remains a fantasy. A survey published in 1988 showed that only 8 per cent of the UK's executive workforce were women.

Equal pay is not yet a reality for most women, mainly because they are still concentrated in low-paid 'female' jobs. A great number of men, whether husbands, fathers or employers, still feel that a woman's place is first and foremost at home, with work as a kind of optional extra, despite the fact that in 1988, 53 per cent of women in Britain went out to work – many of them as the sole supporter of their households. Many families could not survive without a woman's wage.

The assumption continues that an 'ideal' family consists of a wife and children at home, supported by a male breadwinner's 'family wage'; even though such families are in fact now very much in the minority. (Only 5.2 per cent of all households in Britain are like this.) Praise from some politicians in the late 1980s for the idea of this kind of family as an important part of society, has encouraged some people to think it is wrong and altogether 'unnatural' for women to go out to work.

As working women, and those who would like to work,

approach the last decade of the twentieth century, they still face a situation where the world of full-time employment is controlled by, and generally organized for, the needs of men. Women have proved themselves in many walks of life to be as dedicated and competent as the men they work alongside; even so, they are still under-represented in many professions. A girl who wants to be an engineer, a brain surgeon or a train-driver still has to be tough and exceptional in order to make her way. Women at work may have come a long way, but they still have a long way to go.

Projects

1. Draw a timeline or timechart showing the changes in the law affecting women at work during the nineteenth and twentieth centuries. Divide your paper into two by drawing a line, with one narrow column and one wider column. In the narrow column write the date when a certain piece of legislation took place, and in the wider column write the name of the Act of Parliament, along with the good or bad effects it had. You could also include famous strikes and union actions which resulted from certain changes in the law. Look in the 'Books to read' section for books that might be able to help you with historical legislation. For further information on recent and present day laws affecting women in employment you could write to such places as the Equal Opportunities Commission (EOC), the Advisory Conciliation and Arbitration Service (ACAS), as well as the Department of Employment. Addresses for these bodies are:

Information Centre
Equal Opportunities Commission
Overseas House
Quay Street
Manchester M3 3HN

Industrial Relations Information Service (IRIS)
ACAS
27 Wilton Street
London SW1

Department of Employment
Equal Opportunities Unit
Caxton House
Tothill Street
London SW1H 9NF

2. Choose a fairly large factory or office in your area, and try to find out how many women work there, along with the jobs they do. Compare your findings with information about men in the same workplace. Then, with either a pie chart or bar graph, put together the information you have gained. For example, the percentage of women who work in the administration offices, the percentage of women van drivers as compared to men, and so on.

Try to discover any information you can about the history of women's work in your chosen workplace. The local library might be able to help (with newspaper cuttings about the factory), and you could interview any older women workers who might be able to give you some information about what it was like to work there in the past.

3. Think about job titles people have. What image springs to mind when you think of a car mechanic – a man or a woman? Divide a piece of paper into two columns. On one side write down job titles that end in 'man' and on the other those which end in 'woman' or 'lady'. Here are a few examples – gasman, milkman, dustman, coalman, storeman, or tealady, charwoman, dinner lady.

Glossary

Academic subjects Subjects which require reasoned, intellectual knowledge, such as mathematics, English, Latin.

Accomplished Successful or proficient in a certain field, such as music or art etc.

Apprentice Someone who works for a set period with a skilled or qualified person in order to learn a trade or profession.

Billet Lodgings, particularly during wartime, in civilian houses.

Civil Service The service responsible for the public administration of the government.

Compulsory Made to do something by law.

Comradeship Feeling of friendship between a group of people, e.g. workers.

Conscription Compulsory military service.

Conservative A believer in the policies of the Conservative Party – which favours the preservation of established conventional values and beliefs.

Contingent A representative group.

Discrimination Unfair, unjust treatment of a person or group of people on the grounds of sex, race, colour or religion.

Dividend A payment of money from the profit of a company to its shareholders.

Domestic servant A servant employed to help in the home, carrying out most, or all, of the household chores.

Dominated Controlled or governed by someone or something.

Economic recession A period of economic (financial) hardship in a country.

Elementary school Similar to primary school, where the learning of academic subjects begins.

Equal opportunities Equal, advantageous set of circumstances in work between women and men.

Family allowances Similar to our present day Child Benefit, which pays a mother a certain amount of money each week for her child/children under a certain age.

Feminist A person who is determined to improve the position of women in society.

Flexitime A system allowing flexible working hours at the beginning and end of each day, as long as a certain number of hours are completed by the end of the week. Employers usually specify a 'core time' during the day, when employees should be there.

Front Line Military units nearest to fighting.

Independence Freedom, particularly financial, from the control of others.

Industrial Revolution A period in British history, starting around the 1760s, in which the invention of a series of machines, powered by steam, led to a revolution in the way goods were made.

Job sharing Sharing one job between two people. This is particularly suitable for women with young children.

Judicial office Office dealing with administration relating to laws and justice.

Labour Exchange Former name for the Employment Service Agency.

'Living-in' career A job which provides accommodation as well as a wage.

Luddites A group of textile workers opposed to mechanization, who rioted and organized machine-breaking between 1811 and 1816.

'Lying-in' Confinement during and after childbirth.

Minimum wage rates A government-agreed legal minimum wage to be paid to a person for an hour's work.

Misconstrued Wrongly interpreted view or idea.

Misdemeanour A minor offence.

Monopolized Controlled by one or few, with the exclusion of others.

Nationalized An industry that is under state control, rather than privately owned.

Pantry maid A lowly kitchen maid.

Parliamentary reform To change and improve the laws which affect the running and organization of Parliament.

Parlour maid Higher than a pantry maid, a parlour maid, wearing a special uniform, was employed to serve her employers' guests in the formal parlour reception room.

Profession Occupations requiring special training, for example a doctor, lawyer or priest.

Sexual division of labour A theory which holds that women are suited to certain work and men to certain other work.

Shilling A coin which was a unit of currency used in Britain before being replaced by a 5-pence piece in 1970.

Stone-breakers Men and women in the eighteenth and nineteenth century who were employed to break rock into stones by hand.

Subservience Adopting a lower position or attitude.

Substitute To serve temporarily in the place of another person.

Sweatshop Workshop where employees work long hours under bad conditions for low wages.

TNT A yellow solid, used as an explosive.

Trade unions Associations of workers formed to bargain with the employer for better working conditions and pay.

Trapping, hurrying, filling All types of work undertaken in a coal mine.

Tweeny A 'between' maid, who assisted both the cook and the housemaid.

Unity The joining together of separate groups.

Welfare State A government system that seeks to ensure welfare of all citizens under the social services, e.g. the provision of hospitals, family planning, etc.

Books to read

Beddoe, Deirdre *Discovering Women's History: A Practical Manual* (Pandora, 1983)

Beeton, Isobel *Book of Household Management* (1st pub. 1861) (Jonathan Cape, 1968)

Braybon, G. *Women Workers in the First World War* (Croom Helm, 1981)

Cambridge Educational: Women in History Series

Cutting, Pauline *Children of the Siege* (Heinemann, 1988)

Holtby, Winifred *Women in a Changing Civilization* (London, 1934)

John, A.V. *By the Sweat of their Brow: Women Workers at Victorian Coalmines* (Croom Helm, 1980)

Lewis, P. *A People's War* (Methuen, in association with Thames Television International Ltd., 1986)

Longmate, N. (ed.) *The Home Front: an anthology of personal experience 1938–45* (Chatto & Windus, 1981)

Malos, Ellen *The Politics of Housework* (Allison & Busby, 1980)

Marwick, Arthur *Women at War 1914–1918* (Fontana, 1977)

McCrindle, Jean and Rowbotham, Sheila (eds.) *Dutiful Daughters: Women Talk about their Lives* (Penguin, 1979)

Minns, Raynes *Bombers and Mash: The Domestic Front 1939–45* (Virago, 1980)

Noakes, Daisy *The Town Beehive – a young girl's lot, Brighton 1910–34* (QueenSpark Books, Brighton, 1975)

Pollert, A. *Girls, Wives, Factory Lives* (Macmillan, 1981)

Schreiner, Olive *Women and Labour* (Virago, 1978)

Sharpe, S. *Double Identity: The Lives of Working Mothers* (Penguin, 1984)

Spender, D. *Time and Tide Wait for No Man* (Pandora, 1984)

Index

Numbers in **bold** refer to illustrations